DESTROYER.

"Rome will lose the faith and become the seat of the Antichrist."

Apparition of our Blessed Lady in the mountain of La Salette, France 19th of September 1846.*

Thank you...

Thank you God for my life, for what you have giveth me and all the things you have taken away, for all the things you have denied me and all the things you have permitted... You are God, all wisdom, all present, all powerful... Your Love have kept me alive and push me to Love you through all, Thanks for my Lord, your only begotten Son: Jesus, thank you for the Holy Spirit, thank you for our Blessed Mother Mary, for you Holy Archangels and all your Angels, thank you for your special gift the Catholic Church, thank you for your Holy servants: your priests who stand by your Holy word to the death, all your people around the world and your Holy prophets and seers who love you... I thank you for my wife, my 3 children, my mother and all of my family, give us the strength to follow your commands in all things in life and in the brink of crucifixion let us all have the honor to die for your Son and the Holy Gospel. Amen.

Blessings...

God bless you, may God keep you in His Mercy and give you the grace to discern this book in the light of His eternal wisdom.

May the Holy Spirit open your heart, may it cleanse your mind and finally open your eyes to the truth.

May Jesus Christ gives you the thirst to love your enemies, even to those who want to corrupt you to endanger your soul. Jesus loved Judas until his sad end, may Jesus gives you the strength to love despite persecution and horror, like when horror took Him and nailed Him to the cross.

May His sweet Mother Mary teach you to wait and be prepared for the Holy Spirit in the same manner she waited and then she taught the disciples. Amen.

INTRODUCTION

On February 11th 2013, pope Benedict XVI announced his resignation of the papacy, lightning struck the top of the Vatican(1) at 5:55pm...

It has been prophesied, in order for our Lord to come again a rebellion (apostasy), will come forth (2 Thes 2:3).

On March of 2013, Bishop of Argentina: Mario Bergoglio became the new "pope", despite all the murky waters shown by his deeds and words, he was chosen by his peers.

St Francis of Assisi prophecy said of a man non-canonically elected will deceive many, in a time where the sanctity of life will be MOCKED and the IMMACULATE purity of their order will be eclipsed... remember that word: immaculate. St. Francis said in those days a destroyer shall arise.

For Jesus, for the truth kept in His bride the Catholic Church, for my wife, my children, my mother and all my family… for you the Remnant, prayer warriors, Christians, God's children and for those who suffer for the sake of the Kingdom to come… smile, Jesus is coming soon… thanks my dear sister Maria, hopefully I'll see you soon.
Amen.

We begin in the Name of the Father, the Son and the Holy Spirit. Amen.

The prophecy of St Francis of Assisi...

Act bravely, my Brethren[1]; take courage, and trust in the Lord. The time is fast approaching in which there will be great trials and afflictions; perplexities and dissensions, both spiritual and temporal, will abound; the charity of many will grow cold, and the malice of the wicked will increase.

The devils will have unusual power, the immaculate purity of our Order, and of others, will be so much obscured that there will be very few Christians who will obey the true Sovereign Pontiff and the Roman Church with loyal hearts and perfect charity. At the time of this tribulation a man, not canonically elected, will be raised to the Pontificate, who, by his cunning, will endeavour to draw many into error and death.

Then scandals will be multiplied, our Order will be divided, and many others will be entirely destroyed, because they will consent to error instead of opposing it.

There will be such diversity of opinions and schisms among the people, the religious and the clergy, that, except those days were shortened, according to the words of the Gospel, even the elect would be led into error, were they not specially guided, amid such great confusion, by the immense mercy of God.

Then our Rule and manner of life will be violently opposed by some, and terrible trials will come upon us. Those who are found faithful will receive the crown of life; but woe to those who, trusting solely in their Order, shall fall into tepidity, for they will not be able to support the temptations permitted for the proving of the elect.

Those who preserve their fervour and adhere to virtue with love and zeal for the truth, will suffer injuries and, persecutions as rebels and schismatics; for their persecutors, urged on by the evil spirits, will say they are rendering a great service to God by destroying such pestilent men from the face of the earth. But the Lord will be the refuge of the afflicted, and will save all who trust in Him. And in order to be like their Head [Jesus Christ], these, the elect, will act with confidence, and by their death will purchase for themselves eternal life; choosing to obey God rather than man, they will fear nothing, and they will prefer to perish (physically) rather than consent to falsehood and perfidy.

Some preachers will keep silence about the truth, and others will trample it under foot and deny it. Sanctity of life will be held in derision even by those who outwardly profess it, for in those days Jesus Christ will send them not a true Pastor, but a DESTROYER.

Please:

Let's keep in mind, this prophecy of Saint Francis IS approved by the Catholic Church.

Many have defended the man seated upstairs by saying this prophecy is regarding the great schism that gave birth to the orthodox Church...

Not true, is there any other time in history that the truth have been so omitted, trampled, and denied? 1 Billion abortions all around the world since 1980 alone and at the time of the great schism, was sanctity of life so mocked like it is today? Has this prophecy with so many other prophecies of the saints, which have been fulfilled today by the actions, omissions and in your face heresies by Francis and no one saying anything about them like today?

Sad is seeing the blind leading the blind and leading them with a smile, let's begin...

<u>Act bravely, my Brethren; take courage, and trust in the Lord.</u>

It is refreshing seeing our priests, Bishops and Cardinals proclaiming the Gospel with their own lives:

- Card. Raymond Burke
- Card. Pell
- Bishop Athanasius Schneider
- Bishop Livieres
- Fr. Santiago Martin
- Fr. Iglesias
- Fr. Clovis
- The African Catholic Church
- The Polish Catholic Church
- 500+ priests in Wales and Britain
- And many more...

<u>The time is fast approaching in which there will be great trials and afflictions; perplexities and dissensions, both spiritual and temporal, will abound; the charity of many will grow cold, and the malice of the wicked will increase.</u>

We are seeing martyrdom everyday coming closer and closer to our homes, we see in TV how our brethren are killed by those who don't believe in God's Mercy.

ISIS has killed those in live media, but more than 105,000 Christians are being killed each year, and those are numbers which have been statistically unbiased and those numbers don't reflect, the abuse we don't know, but only God sees, blood is bathing the streets of those who don't truly believe, but Jesus is calling us to pray for them with true charity.

<u>The devils will have unusual power, the IMMACULATE purity of our Order, and of others, will be so much obscured that there will be very few Christians who will obey the true Sovereign Pontiff and the Roman Church with loyal hearts and perfect charity.</u>

When pope Benedict XVI resigned I felt like I was been stripped from something, I truly felt naked in the streets, my tears fell down for a man who wasn't popular.

Every Catholic in the world felt that he was pushed out the door despite him assuring he was resigning freely.

Mario Bergoglio came forth and the first thing that caught my attention despite all the prophecies, the hammering of the Franciscans of the IMMACULATE[3].

Remember that word? IMMACULATE? The Franciscans of the immaculate were the most healthy order in the entire Catholic Church, the had more vocations than any order. They wanted to live the PURITY of what their creator (St. Francis of Assisi), wanted... to be poor, do charity, penance, and love our Lord through the old mass.

Mario Bergoglio came forth and despite having many heresies under his belt in the past, like letting his beloved 'curas villeros' to give the Eucharist to irregular couples[4], letting a priest to baptized the child of a transvestite couple with a belly for hire[5] and the "let's allow gay unions, without calling it marriage" in a meeting with the bishops of Argentina[6]... despite all that, he was chosen by his peers to seat in the throne of Peter.

He called himself Francis and the first thing he does is fulfilling the prophecy of St Francis of Assisi by reengineering the Franciscans of the Immaculate, that's when I opened my eyes...

I remember asking my priest why pope Francis said:

"Atheists do good and well meet there"[7]

My priest said "Maybe he didn't had his breakfast that morning" Well, he has said a lot of those and I assure that he eats well.

IMMACULATE... the destruction was warned by St Francis of Assisi, the destruction would began there!

Poor pope Benedict XVI his legacy thrown to the ground, God bless his sweet soul. Amen.

At the time of this tribulation a man, not canonically elected, will be raised to the Pontificate, who, by his cunning, will endeavour to draw many into error and death.

Many have already talked about this:

Antonio Socci... claims that Bergoglio's election was invalid, because the laws of the Apostolic Constitution "Universi Dominici Gregis" governing voting in the Sistine Chapel weren't followed.(*)

Sandro Magister... shows how the 'curas villeros' gave the Eucharist to irregular couples in the slums of Argentina, under the protection of Bergoglio, this is a sacrilege and it is sufficient enough to enter into effect the law described by St. Robert Bellarmine, which speaks clearly that anyone being a heretic can't be pope even with the majority of votes.(**)

Dr. Austen Ivereigh... In his book, "The great reformer: Francisco and the manufacture of a radical pope" in the encyclical Universi Dominici Gregis, promulgated by Pope John Paul II in 1996, says that lobbying for votes is strictly prohibited before the conclave to elect the next pope, with the penalty of automatic excommunication. In his book Dr. Ivereigh shows how the head of the "Bergoglio team", tried to lobby for at least 25 votes to start the conclave and it was confirmed in the interviews given by the head of the Bergoglio team: Cardinal Murphy O'Connor in The Wall Street Journal (08/06/2013) and in the Catholic Herald (2013).(***)

These 3 journalists have impeccable reputation, and according to Dr. Ivereigh, the Bergoglio team tried in 2005 to make Bergoglio pope, but Joseph Ratzinger got elected.

The Holy Spirit prevailed and Almighty Father will came out to bless the people as Benedict XVI, this evil team started since 2005 with the full knowledge of Bergoglio, each and every one of them were excommunicated automatically, they, in their disobedience, were cut out from the mystical body of Jesus and through the words of Bergoglio, and the many liberalist seated in positions of power, it only shows how our Church is under attack from within by the enemy, trying to corrupt the Holy Temple and in this way the antichrist could waltz in like a hero and declare that he is god.

<u>Then scandals will be multiplied, our Order will be divided, and many others will be entirely destroyed, because they will consent to error instead of opposing it.</u>

Scandals, that's all you have since also Jesus had amongst the disciples a traitor, in order for Rome to 'lose its faith' as our Blessed Mother foretold in La Salette, the Holy Temple needs to be corrupted, so scandals are a priority for the devil and his minions.

Today it is taught by the top, that it doesn't matter if you're gay, because "If someone is gay and he searches for the Lord and has good will, who am I to judge?"[8]

For faithful Catholics, in other words, those who know their faith, the appointments of the Bruno Forte's of the world ARE a huge scandal and

Mario Bergoglio doesn't care and is noted because of the many Kumbaya appointments been laid, like it's some sort of a chess match, liberals in all high places and the appointment of a liberal alone it is a door for the ruin of souls in hell.

Popes of the past have appointed bad apples but they rely on advice for some of the appointments, while the papacy moves forth, but... the servants of God, the consecrated they're supposed to see more easily the wolves in sheep clothing than the laity, and Bergoglio has appointed the many liberalists in high places, so yes, he knows what he is doing, he was a liberalist himself in Argentina.

A man who fought for marriage in the Argentinean congress, but when he had meetings with the gay communities, he apologizes because he had many "enemies" in the Church(6).

His fruits says it all about his past agenda with gays and today even more, as he kissed the hand of famous gay mass priest(9) and stood silent while Ireland change her name to Sodom(10).

So yes error definitely is been accepted in silence, slowly but steady... yes the Franciscans have abandoned tradition for the anti-gospel, the 30 coins gospel: The World and its fruits.

Franciscans embracing error where? At a gay parade in Boston.(11)

<u>There will be such diversity of opinions and schisms among the people, the religious and the clergy, that, except those days were shortened, according to the words of the Gospel, even the elect would be led into error, were they not specially guided, amid such great confusion, by the immense mercy of God.</u>

Confusion is the main goal of the enemy for those who are of God, the enemy would love for all of the Christian world to be confused in such a way, that their souls could be in danger, by failing to work their salvation in fear and in tremble (Phil 2:12).

Nuns singing in competitions), nuns walking the streets without their habits, priests proclaiming in their homilies to vote for Gay equality[12] and how they put sin like nothing.

Laity rejecting dogma, for respect with the falsity: "As long I don't harm anyone is all good", a society driven to respect all religions except Christianity and those in Israel.

What was Good yesterday now is bad, and what's Good today was bad yesterday… GLOBAL APOSTASY!

The only thing that will lead us away from error is to obey God rather than men (Acts 5:29), God's commands, His Holy Word doesn't contradict itself. God loves us but despises sin, don't be deceive God's Mercy is for those who repent and seek perfection walking with Jesus to Calvary.

<u>Then our Rule and manner of life will be violently opposed by some, and terrible trials will come upon us. Those who are found faithful will receive the crown of life; but woe to those who, trusting solely in their Order, shall fall into tepidity, for they will not be able to support the temptations permitted for the proving of the elect.</u>

The tridentine mass is been persecuted by the devil since long, and it was the old mass that the Franciscans of the Immaculate embraced.

Jesus is the same yesterday, today and forever (Heb 13:8), if the Franciscans of yesterday loved the tridentine mass, and the Franciscans of today (those who have embrace the purity of the Franciscan rule – Franciscans of the Immaculate), embrace the Latin mass, why stop them? Because the world hates those who are contrary to its ruler: the devil.

This is why I truly believe that Archbishop Marcel Lefebvre is a saint (the SSPX - even though I don't have them in my beloved St. Petersburg), Bishop Lefebvre has kept the traditions of the one true Church intact, God bless them!

But we also have Champions in our everyday catholic life as the Tridentine mass still happens with so much persecution.

The Latin mass is heaven's mass and the new mass is a sacrifice with the full process of crucifixion, where the chaff and the wheat is recognizable and soon, through this mass and the apostasy set by the top, the abomination of desolation shall take place:

"From the time that the daily sacrifice is abolished and the desolating abomination is set up, there shall be one thousand two hundred and ninety days". (Daniel 12:11).

<u>Those who preserve their fervour and adhere to virtue with love and zeal for the truth, will suffer injuries and, persecutions as rebels and schismatics; for their persecutors, urged on by the evil spirits, will say they are rendering a great service to God by destroying such pestilent men from the face of the earth.</u>

This part of the prophecy of St Francis of Assisi is on the horizon, this our future, for those who persevere... heaven in a silver platter:

MARTYRDOM!

"I expected to die in bed, my successor will die in prison and his successor will die a martyr in the public square." Cardinal George (Ora pro nobis)(13)

Now let's pray for Cardinal George successor (Bishop Cupich), embraces Christ, because he is giving the Eucharist to abortionists(14), so let's pray that if indeed there's a little bit of prophecy in Card. George words (and I truly believe they were prophetic despite he said the contrary), pray for him to go to jail for the right reasons (Gospel wise speaking), because there's too many people preaching error in the most beautiful words to confuse the laity.

Those who die standing for the truth written in the Gospel, will have eternity, so soon we shall see who is chaff and who is wheat. God give us the gift of perseverance and please you in all your commandments. Amen.

<u>But the Lord will be the refuge of the afflicted, and will save all who trust in Him. And in order to be like their Head [Jesus Christ], these, the elect, will act with confidence, and by their death will purchase for themselves eternal life; choosing to obey God rather than man, they will fear nothing, and they will prefer to perish (physically) rather than consent to falsehood and perfidy.</u>

This part of the prophecy is for all who follow the Lord of Lords, Jesus... people who are true believers in His Mercy.

He has given us the path of Mercy through the traditions and teachings laid by Him through His disciples and Patriarchs.

NO Bishop, pope or antipope can change one single coma of His Holy Word. (Gal 1:8)

The Eucharist and all the sacraments are to be proclaimed, and the faithful shall pray for the salvation of souls:

"Brothers, my heart's desire and prayer to God for them is that they may be saved." (Romans 10:1)

The Rosary, the Divine Mercy Chaplet and the St. Michael's prayer are to be recite for a world full of disbelief for them to embrace the everlasting Mercy of God.

All approve devotions are accepted but one prayer with love beats whatever prayer with no love... so love till it hurts! Amen.

<u>Some preachers will keep silence about the truth, and others will trample it under foot and deny it. Sanctity of life will be held in derision even by those who outwardly profess it, for in those days Jesus Christ will send them not a true Pastor, but a DESTROYER.</u>

Truth has received all kinds of omission while been trampled upon by the top, is like, there's a fear for a career, when St Athanasius today is a Saint despite excommunication by a pope.

We the laity need to know that we shouldn't follow ANYONE, who is a liberalist and seeks to please the world, better yet... we need to pray for their souls, NOT their intentions.

Would you pray for the intentions of a thief before the throne of God?

If anyone preaches a worldly and liberalist gospel, we know their intentions aren't good, if we do, despite knowing they are a wolf in sheep clothing, then we are guilty of evil.

Soon the destroyer called by St Francis of Assisi will called for Mercy for the "Lepers" of the world and will try to change the Church for the sake of false Mercy, as the homosexuals and the divorce and re-married are meant to receive the Eucharist because the Eucharist "is not for the perfect... but for the weak."[15]

The destroyer has mocked the sanctity of life many times but is all fun and games to most... "We talk too much about abortion, homosexuality and contraception"[16] and "Don't breed like rabbits"[17] is all for laughter, God is not laughing... open your eyes, soon Francis will try to change things for the sake of the "weak", but even the poor needs the Holy Word of God instead of goods.

The Franciscans of the Immaculate have shown through the prophecy of St Francis of Assisi, how the destruction would began and people who don't know their faith are embracing confusion like the most sweet honey, Christ never spoke ex-cathedra and even Bergoglio has said that his homilies are "teachings."[19]

Destroyer, because many will fall, many souls will follow the "who am I to judge", that phrase alone is responsible for many people embracing liberalism as Mercy, when Mercy without Justice is like Love without truth.

Open your eyes and don't follow the wolves, remain faithful while resisting and pray with love for all of those who wants to destroy us, but not for their intentions.

"Watch out for false prophets. They come to you in sheep's clothing, but inwardly they are ferocious wolves. By their fruit you will recognize them. Do people pick grapes from thornbushes, or figs from thistles? Likewise, every good tree bears good fruit, but a bad tree bears bad fruit. A good tree cannot bear bad fruit, and a bad tree cannot bear good fruit." (Mat 7:15-19)

For those Catholics who should
know more about their faith...

It is in the Bible that our Lord warn us about those who are wolves in sheep clothing and many saints and doctors of the Church has spoken about it to the laity, for us NOT to follow any pope who has abandoned the truth in any way, either by heresy, omission, and destruction(1):

<u>Apostle Peter:</u> "But Peter and the apostles answering, said: We ought to obey God, rather than men." (Acts 5:29)

<u>Doctor Saint Thomas Aquinas:</u> "It is written: '*We ought to obey God rather than men.*' Now sometimes the things commanded by a superior are against God. Therefore, superiors are NOT to be obeyed in all things." (Summa Theologiae, IIa IIae, Q. 104, A. 5)

<u>St Paul:</u> "But when Cephas [Peter] was come to Antioch, I withstood him to the face, because he was to be blamed." (Galatians 2:11)

<u>Pope Innocent III:</u> "The pope should not flatter himself about his power, nor should he rashly glory in his honour and high estate, because the less he is judged by man, the more he is judged by God. Still the less can the Roman Pontiff glory, because he can be judged by men, or rather, can be shown to be already judged, if for example he should wither away into heresy, because *"he who does not believe is already judged."* (St. John 3:18) In such a case it should be said of him: *'If salt should lose its savour, it is good for nothing but to be cast out and trampled under foot by men.'"* (Sermo 4)

<u>Venerable Pope Pius IX:</u> "If a future pope teaches anything contrary to the Catholic Faith, do not follow him." (Letter to Bishop Brizen)

St. Athanasius: "Even if Catholics faithful to Tradition are reduced to a handful, they are the ones who are the true Church of Jesus Christ." (Epistle to the Catholics)

St. Vincent of Lerins: "What then should a Catholic do if some portion of the Church detaches itself from communion of the universal Faith? What choice can he make if some new contagion attempts to poison, no longer a small part of the Church, but the whole Church at once? Then his great concern will be to attach himself to antiquity which can no longer be led astray by any lying novelty." (Commonitory)

Council Vatican I (1870): "For the Holy Ghost was promised to the successors of Peter NOT so that they might, by His revelation, make known some new doctrine, but that, by His assistance, they might religiously guard and faithfully expound the revelation or Deposit of Faith transmitted by the Apostles." (Pastor Aeternus, cap. 4)

<u>Doctor of the Church, St. Robert Bellarmine:</u> "Just as it is lawful to resist the pope that attacks the body, it is also lawful to resist the one who attacks souls or who disturbs civil order, or, above all, who attempts to **destroy the Church**. I say that it is lawful to resist him by not doing what he orders and preventing his will from being executed." (De Romano Pontifice, Lib. II, Ch. 29)

The Secret...

Blessed Catherine Emmerich, AA II. 488.(1)

"I saw within a city, a meeting of clergy, laymen and women, who were sitting together, eating and making frivolous jokes, and above them a dark cloud which descended in a plain submerged in darkness. Amid this fog, I saw Satan sitting and around him, many companions as people were in the meeting which was going on underneath. All these evil spirits were continually moving and busy trying to push the people at this meeting to do evil. They whispered to them to their ears and acted on them in all possible ways.

These people were in a very dangerous state of sensual excitement and in provocative conversations. Churchmen were those whose principle were: "You have to LIVE AND LET LIVE. In our time we should not be apart or be a misanthrope: we must rejoice with those who rejoice."

This is one of the many visions by Blessed Catherine Emmerich (1774-1824), who suffered much during her lifetime for the love of Christ and His Church... she was beatified by Saint pope John Paul II.

In July 27th 2014 the man seated in Peter's throne gave an interview and released to the world the top 10 secrets to be happy[2]:

1) LIVE AND LET LIVE.

The other 9 secrets to happiness by Bergoglio are just humanistic in nature, in other words, constructed for the elect to become less religion minded and more world minded people, why? Do know this: there's no mention of Jesus anywhere...

2) Be giving of yourself to others." People need to be open and generous toward others, he said, because "if you withdraw into yourself, you run the risk of becoming egocentric. And stagnant water becomes putrid."
3) "Proceed calmly" in life. The pope, who used to teach high school literature, used an image from an Argentine novel by Ricardo Guiraldes, in which the protagonist-- gaucho Don Segundo Sombra-- looks back on how he lived his life.

"He says that in his youth he was a stream full of rocks that he carried with him; as an adult, a rushing river; and in old age, he was still moving, but slowly, like a pool" of water, the pope said. He said he likes this latter image of a pool of water -- to have "the ability to move with kindness and humility, a calmness in life."
4) "A healthy sense of leisure." "A healthy sense of leisure." The pleasures of art,

literature and playing together with children have been lost, he said.

"Consumerism has brought us anxiety" and stress, causing people to lose a "healthy culture of leisure." Their time is "swallowed up" so people can't share it with anyone.

Even though many parents work long hours, they must set aside time to play with their children; work schedules make it "complicated, but you must do it," he said.

Families must also turn off the TV when they sit down to eat because, even though television is useful for keeping up with the news, having it on during mealtime "doesn't let you communicate" with each other, the pope said.

5) Sundays should be holidays. Workers should have Sundays off because "Sunday is for family," he said.
6) Find innovative ways to create dignified jobs for young people. "We need to be creative with young people. If they have

no opportunities they will get into drugs" and be more vulnerable to suicide, he said.

"It's not enough to give them food," he said. "Dignity is given to you when you can bring food home" from one's own labor.

7) Respect and take care of nature. Environmental degradation "is one of the biggest challenges we have," he said. "I think a question that we're not asking ourselves is: 'Isn't humanity committing suicide with this indiscriminate and tyrannical use of nature?'"

8) Stop being negative. "Needing to talk badly about others indicates low self-esteem. That means, 'I feel so low that instead of picking myself up I have to cut others down,'" the pope said. "Letting go of negative things quickly is healthy."

9) Don't proselytize; respect others' beliefs. "We can inspire others through witness so that one grows together in communicating. But the worst thing of all is religious proselytism, which

paralyzes: 'I am talking with you in order to persuade you,' No. Each person dialogues, starting with his and her own identity. The church grows by attraction, not proselytizing," the pope said.

10) Work for peace. "We are living in a time of many wars," he said, and "the call for peace must be shouted. Peace sometimes gives the impression of being quiet, but it is never quiet, peace is always proactive" and dynamic.

This first "secret" fulfills the vision of Blessed Catherine Emmerich about a certain gathering where the "talks" were provocative and dangerous, this gathering happened in the first Synod of the family where a wicked relatio was given and quotes like[3]:

<u>"Homosexuals have gifts and qualities to offer to the Christian community". "Are we capable of welcoming these people, guaranteeing to them a fraternal space in our communities? "</u>

(n.50). Although not comparing unions between the same sexes to marriage between a man and woman, the Church proposes to: "elaborate realistic paths of affective growth and human and evangelical maturity integrating the sexual dimension" (n.51) "Without denying the moral problems connected to homosexual unions it has to be noted that there are cases in which mutual aid to the point of sacrifice constitutes a precious support in the life of the partners." (n.52).

No moral objection was made on the adoption of children by homosexual couples: all that was said was "the Church pays special attention to the children who live with couples of the same sex, emphasizing that the needs and rights of the little ones must always be given priority."

So yes, it seems that Bergoglio is having a blast fulfilling prophecies of the Saints left and right.

Blessed Catherine Emmerich, pray for us. Amen.

Contradictions

Pope Francis: "Atheists do good and we'll meet one another there..." On 5/22/2013, homily at Santa Marta.(1)

Jesus: "Whoever does not believe will be condemned..." John 3:18

Pope Francis: "Christians with the Bible, Muslims with the Quran with the faith of your fathers that it will take you far." On 01/20/2014 pope Francis visited the Sacred Heart Basilica at Castro Pretorio, and there he share this with the youth.(2)

St Paul: "But even if we or an angel from heaven should preach [to you] a gospel other than the one that we preached to you, let that one be accursed." Gal 1:8

Pope Francis: "I rebuked a woman some months ago in a parish who was pregnant eight times, with seven C-sections. 'But do you want to leave seven orphans?' This is to tempt God! He [Paul VI] speaks of responsible parenthood." Not content with rebuking this particular woman, he extends it worldwide: "God gives you methods to be responsible. Some think that, excuse me if I use that word, that in order to be good Catholics we have to be like rabbits. No. Responsible parenthood! This is clear and that is why in the church there are marriage groups, there are experts in this matter, there are pastors, one can seek and I know so many, many ways out that are licit and that have helped this." On 01/19/2015 in the plane back to Rome from the Philippines.(3)

God Almighty: "Be fruitful and multiply." Gen 1:28

Pope Francis: "Proselytism is a solemn nonsense." On Oct. 2013 during the Scalfari interview for newspaper La Republica, he also repeat this to an interview to Viva Magazine on 07/27/2014.(4)

Jesus: "Make disciples of all Nations" Mat 28:19.

Pope Francis: "Jesus pretended." On 11/29/2013 Homily at Santa Marta Jesus was called a pretender in other words a liar.(5)

Jesus: "I am the way, the truth and the life." John 14:6

Pope Francis: "We talk too much about abortion, contraception and homosexuality." On September, 2013 Fr Spadaro interview.(6)

St. Paul: "Do not be carried away by all kind of strange teachings." Heb 13:9

Pope Francis: "If my good friend Doctor Gasparri [who organises the Pope's trips] speaks badly of my mother, he can expect to get punched. You cannot provoke. You cannot insult the faith of others. You cannot make fun of the faith of others. There is a limit." On 01/19/2015 in the plane back to Rome from the Philippines.(7)

Jesus: "To the person who strikes you on one cheek, offer the other one as well, and from the person who takes your cloak, do not withhold even your tunic." Luke 6:29

Pope Francis: "If someone is gay and he searches for the Lord and has good will, who am I to judge?" On 7/29/13 in an interview by reporters on the plane back from the world youth in Brazil, back to Rome.(8)

St. Paul: "Do you not know that the unjust will not inherit the kingdom of God? Do not be deceived; neither fornicators nor idolaters nor adulterers nor boy prostitutes nor sodomites nor thieves nor the greedy nor drunkards nor slanderers nor robbers will inherit the kingdom of God." 1 Cor 6:9-10

Pope Francis: "The old pact with the Jews is not broken." Evangelii Gaudium #247
(Note: If the pact is not broken then they don't need Jesus)(9)

God Almighty: "See, days are coming—oracle of the LORD—when I will make a new covenant with the house of Israel and the house of Judah It will not be like the covenant I made with their ancestors the day I took them by the hand to lead them out of the land of Egypt. They broke my covenant, though I was their master—oracle of the LORD But this is the covenant I will make with the house of Israel after those days—oracle of the LORD. I will place my law within them, and write it upon their hearts; I will be their God, and they shall be my people." Jer 31:31-33

Pope Francis: "It is beautiful "to think of Heaven," "All of us will meet there, everyone. It is beautiful; it gives strength to the soul." On Nov. 2014 at a general audience in St Peter's square.(10)

Jesus: "Strive to enter through the narrow door, for many, I tell you, will attempt to enter but will not be strong enough." Luke 13:24

Pope Francis: "Don't fear final judgment." On 12/11/2013 at a general audience in St Peter's square.(11)

St Paul: "So then, my beloved, obedient as you have always been, not only when I am present but all the more now when I am absent, work out your salvation with fear and trembling." Phil 2:12

Pope Francis: "Sundays should be holidays. Workers should have Sundays off because "Sunday is for family."
Interview to Viva Magazine on 07/27/2014.(12)

St Paul: On the first day of the week, when we were gathered together to break bread, Paul talked with them, intending to depart on the next day, and he prolonged his speech until midnight." Acts 20:7

Evangelii Gaudium opens the door to abortion

What would happen with the soul of a mother who was raped or someone in conditions of extreme poverty, who, gets an abortion and suddenly dies after murdering the child, hold that thought for a moment.

There are 48,198 words in Evangelii Gaudium (without the notes), in which you will find lots and lots of beautiful words, you could find love mentioned more than 150 times, God 290 times, Jesus 125 times, Mary 37 times, church 233 times, mercy 30 and it goes on and on...

We can't deny it, Evangelii Gaudium is beautiful in its literature...

Now, there are words that you won't find in Evangelii Gaudium, you won't find HELL, DEMONS, DIVORCE, HOMOSEXUAL, LESBIAN, GAY, CONTRACEPTION...

The Catholic Church main mission is to save souls and it is troublesome when people of the church are in line to hide the truth, because offering one truth and hiding another can lead people to the very same place that is not mentioned here, HELL.

"We cannot insist only on issues related to abortion, gay marriage and the use of contraceptive methods. This is not possible. I have not spoken much about these things, and I was reprimanded for that. But when we speak about these issues, we have to talk about them in a context. The teaching of the church, for that matter, is clear and I am a son of the church, but it is not necessary to talk about these issues all the time."[1]

Pope Francis gave an interview in which he said that the church is obsessed with contraception, homosexuality and abortion; abortion is only mentioned once... let me repeat that again ONCE; even though in n.213 Francis writes beautifully about the defense of the unborn children and about the Church defending human rights, in n.214 he mentions for the first time ABORTION:

214. Precisely because this involves the internal consistency of our message about the value of the human person, the Church cannot be expected to change her position on this question. I want to be completely honest in this regard. This is not something subject to alleged reforms or "modernizations". It is not "progressive" to try to resolve problems by eliminating a human life. On the other hand, it is also true that we have done little to adequately accompany women in very difficult situations, where

ABORTION APPEARS AS A QUICK SOLUTION to their profound anguish, especially when the life developing within them is the result of rape or a situation of extreme poverty. Who can remain unmoved before such painful situations?(2)

If the enemy is at the gates and you open the door just a little bit, it'll be more easier for them to push their way in, everything that Francis wrote about defending the unborn in both n.213 and 214, goes out the window when you make such statement.

Every effort of the church about abortion has been thrown to the ground with this piece of beautiful literature, literature that could take souls to hell.

What would happen with those who follows this advice? What about those in the hands of whoever performs the abortion?

What if the mother suddenly dies? What about that soul?

God's Mercy is the twin sister of God's Justice, whenever one goes the other is there, for much Mercy we preach we can't deny Justice, by giving such erroneous advice people could go to eternal damnation, there are many scenarios that we could play, many "God is the one who judges", yes of course... but if we are saving souls, we teach to stay away from MORTAL SIN.

Are we following Christ through the Catholic Church in its apostolic teachings, or is this mass hysteria? Is the world finally getting the Church to do what the world wants?

Sin only appears written 10 times and the word devil just once... ONCE!

When Francis spoke about the devil, he was referring about the traditionalists in the Church (read n.83), tradition accepted and embraced by every saint in the church, you can see the persecution to traditionalists all around the world and recently to one of the champions against abortion, Cardinal Raymond Burke.[3]

There are many conflicting messages in the Evangelii Gaudium, like both n.168 and n.271 in which denouncing error and evil it's a problem, n.47 which is against about the practice of denying communion to people who persists in their wickedness, n.247 which says that the Jewish people still has the old pact intact, and many more.

What is all of this? What is the purpose of my words? Many things:

1) We need to pray for all of our priests and pray for clarity in this times of confusion.

2) We need to know that there's a slowly but steady persecution to pro-lifers within our own church and this n.214 says with subtleness, that their future inside the church is doomed – pray for the pro-lifers.

3) Our own church is persecuting anyone which loves tradition (example: the Franciscans of the immaculate) – pray for all of them.

4) Many are in line with this new Church of the world, instead of the teachings of the true bride of Christ and this people will defend this new Kumbaya Gospel...

Remember a truth with a lie is a lie altogether (the Qur'an is a good example). Please, my intention is to reveal the truth and denounce error, again... error can lead souls to hell and hell is one place that Jesus Himself speaks more than anyone in the bible.

Pray with me: "Oh Mary conceived without sin pray to your Son our Lord Jesus Christ to change the waters of our lives into another color, turn Lord Jesus like you did in Cana the waters of our lives into wine, so our lives could have another color, the color of your Love." Amen.

Pope Francis: "The sacredness of the human person"

A take on the most humanistic speech ever by a "pope" (Pope Francis at the EU parliament)(1)

On November 25th, 2014 Pope Francis obeyed our Lord Jesus and told the Parliament to convert to our Savior and Lord Jesus Christ like our forefathers use to do when faced with Emperors, Kings, generals and the Jewish elite... Not...!

My apologies for the sarcasm... Sorry, but I am hurt, sad and deeply troubled with this "pope of the end of the world" words, deeds and borderline heresies, I just want to close my eyes and forget, there's someone out there seating at the Top who is behaving more and more like he's from other religion, like someone back in Israel (when he visited Israel), said:

"The pope is more focus on saving the world, not souls."

Pope Francis visited the EU parliament and if it was the president, dictator or politician of some country trying to gain political points with the Elite and powerful, I would've understand, but not from a pope.

> *"I believe, therefore, that it is vital to develop a culture of human rights which wisely links the individual, or better, the personal aspect, to that of the common good, of the 'all of us"* Pope Francis

The common good, it feels like we are in some Star Trek episode... The pope used many beautiful words, as he did with his Joy of the Gospel which is beautiful in words but deadly in its ambiguity.

Pope Francis said the most Humanism base speech that I have ever heard from anyone, he utilized in his 6 page speech the word human 29 times: human dignity, human rights, beings, person, nature, life, spirit, family, ecology, development, value and of course humanity and humanism.

It wasn't like pope St John Paul the great as pope Benedict once called him, when pope John Paul talked to the Parliament in 1988 about Blessed Niels Stensen constantly seeking for the truth... but for Francis? No, it was more about providing "dignity for the human person"

> *"Promoting the dignity of the person means recognizing that he or she possesses inalienable rights which no one may take away arbitrarily, much less for the sake of economic interests." Pope Francis.*

Many words for the sake of a better world were made, rights for all, providing for the needy, education, immigration, etc... but the reality yesterday, today and tomorrow is

Jesus, without Jesus Christ, without calling to repent and convert, not assuring the nations that true peace can only be achieve by trusting the Lord Jesus Christ, by not saying that at the EU, then there is nothing, emptiness.

In Francis speech he mentioned the word Jesus, zero times... the same can be said for salvation, convert, truth, freedom, worship, euthanasia, hell, devil, abortion, contraception and homosexuality, of course...

This pope is more on the humanism side than the spiritual side, he has said it himself, "religious proselytism is a solemn nonsense", he mentioned the word God 4 times and Lord 1 time... and of course with no intention to convert anyone, also you could say, he, by saying God and Lord will be suffice, but Francis doesn't want to offend anyone by proclaiming Jesus as Lord and Savior in front of the world... why would he? I mean he said it himself... "I don't believe in a Catholic God, I believe in God"

Muslims believe in God, Jehovah's witness believe in God, Buddhists believe in God and even some lower level freemasons believe in God, but only the Catholic Church has a Savior and God, Jesus... so yes He is an Universal God, a Catholic God, the only begotten Son of Almighty Father.

Only the truth shall set us free said the Lord, like how it did to Blessed Niels Stensen, born as a protestant, converted, became a priest, a scientist, a Bishop, a zealous defender and lover of the Eucharist...

> "There is only one human response to the self-giving love which shows itself on the cross and lives in the Church as

the true bread of humanity,' *Blessed Niels Stensen*(2)

Pray for pope Francis conversion, pray for his soul to accept Jesus Christ to please our Lord in ALL His commandments, DO NOT pray for Francis intentions, as he has made clear that he is more for the "reality" of the world...

"Dear Members of the European Parliament, the time has come to work together in building a Europe which revolves not around the economy, but around the sacredness of the human person, around inalienable values." Pope Francis.

Pray with me: "Forgive me Jesus I love you, I embrace your Love, I embrace the Son of God, I embrace my cross, I embrace your Kingdom and deny the world now. Amen

False Mercy

False Mercy is by simple definition the contrary of Divine Mercy and Divine Mercy is love acting for us, Divine love from the offended which is God to the transgressors which is us, so... False mercy is just that, action build to deceive.

False is something that is not true, something that doesn't hold at all, is something that looks, sounds, feels or smells real but at the same time is not. When falseness combines with Mercy the definition becomes a little broader, it is a set of things, because Mercy is one thing us humans seek to heal our souls, to silence or guilt and reach out to God to welcome us back, something we need to feel at peace, it is the Light of God and without we are in darkness.

Darkness today feels normal, the world is entirely in darkness, it is run by darkness, but our souls are made in God's image and what belongs to God needs God, so when Mercy is preached immediately creates in us the spiritual urge to embrace it, as we are spiritual beings, but we are blinded by the world and by our very flesh, so False Mercy becomes attractive when we hear what our flesh wants to hear.

A homosexual who hears "who am I to judge"[1] feels relieved, their conscience goes into a "relative" peace, because they have been told all of their lives, "your behavior is wrong, wicked, the bible tells it so, homosexuality is not only a sin, but an abomination" (Lev 20:13) [2], calming people consciences are not the job of who are preaching Mercy, but to tell you the truth so you can find the light of God.

"...For this I was born and for this I came into the world, to testify to the truth. Everyone who belongs to the truth listens to my voice." John 18:37

False Mercy is what you want to hear, to relieve your conscience and that "peace" is just a lie... you see, a lie or falseness with tiny pieces of truth is a lie altogether, Homosexuality, divorce and re-married, stealing to a thief, doing borderline wrong, seeing sin as nothing, that we are all save, all of this, without true repentance is False Mercy.

When His excellency Bishop Fellay told the world about those who preach false Mercy to people:

"...by telling them there is an open door when there is none. The door that is being opened is a door to hell! These prelates who have received the power of the keys, that is, of opening the gates of Heaven, are closing them, and opening the gates of hell." [3]

Many started helping false Mercy with the "respect" card, by not saying the truth, those who don't say the truth are harming those who belong to God, by not knowing the truth they stay in sin and after death, sin with no repentance, can open the doors of hell; truth will set you free (John 8:32) [4] said the Lord, because total truth will make you want to rethink, you either embrace the truth and repent (John 18:37) or you'll reject truth and continue in your sin.

False Mercy has the whole world and the devil protecting it with a call of bigotry, lack of understanding, sometimes calling people haters and legalists, even if you are denouncing the wicked acts, not who commits them, they say that you are judging people, when you are proclaiming the Gospel, because you are only repeating what God says and the world don't like it, hate for those who proclaim the truth.

"If the world hates you, realize that it hated me first. If you belonged to the world, the world would love its own; but because you do not belong to the world, and I have chosen you out of the world, the world hates you. John 15:18-19

But the world needs those who proclaim the Gospel to become corrupt and preach false Mercy, so many souls relax about seeking perfection and because the flesh has the urge to sin and you can't control yourself, then you sin, but with false Mercy is alright, because God "understands"... God doesn't give a law to then ignore His own law **don't be deceive**.

People want to embrace false Mercy because it gives you what your flesh needs, it calms your conscience with exactly what you want to hear, not what your soul truly needs, this is why many embrace strange teachings and many pastors are happy to give it, because they are blinded themselves out of their own sin, sin they believe don't exist or believe that God "understands" and forgives you automatically.

False Mercy is on the outside beautiful and attractive, way too easy and way too mundane... Loving the Lord is hard, following His commandments only creates enemies and pure hate from those you use to love or those who come to know you, despite that, follow the Lord and don't despair, don't hold a grudge... continue to love truth and trust the Lord.

Reject False Mercy, reject darkness, reject the devil and his works, many will say he doesn't exist but he does, and many will fight to protect him even un-knowingly FIGHT, fight, fight... your Lord Jesus is with you, nothing will harm you, even those who claim to be His apostles, preachers of falseness, look at their fruits, their bad fruits and you'll know them, false prophets (Mat 7:15-16) reject darkness, may the Lord give us the grace to repent and love Him perfectly in truth. Amen

Pope Benedict draws a line in the sand...

In a written message to The Pontifical Urbaniana University in Rome, Pope Emeritus Benedict XVI emphasized that the renunciation of truth is "lethal to faith,"[1]

"Many today think religions should respect each other and, in their dialogue, become a common force for peace," the Pope Emeritus continued. "The question of truth, that which originally motivated Christians more than any other, is here put inside parentheses... This renunciation of truth seems realistic and useful for peace among religions in the world."

"...is nevertheless lethal to faith"

"loses its binding character and its seriousness, everything is reduced to interchangeable symbols, capable of referring only distantly to the inaccessible mystery of the divine."

What is the sole mission of the Church? Save souls and make saints...

Pope Francis has declare a lot of borderline heresies and has acted in such a way, that you don't know if he is for the Lord Jesus or for another strange religion. Benedict can't say that, if the Faith is threaten with what many wolves in sheep clothing are preaching and lobbying for today, we can't see Benedict not doing what any good disciple of our Lord would do... point out what's wrong, and if not heard, if those who are for the world don't change, then distance yourself from iniquity.

As for a person who stirs up division, after warning him once and then twice, have nothing more to do with him, knowing that such a person is warped and sinful; he is self-condemned. Titus 3:10-11

Cardinal Burke has called the wrongs, Archbihop Ganswein, Archbishop Athanasius Schneider, Bishop Gadecki and some others too and pope Benedict has produced a written message and corrected his own writings for Francis own cardinal Kasper, for him NOT to use pope Benedict's words, on lobbying the lie from hell: divorce and re-married communion.

Pope Benedict XVI has called NOT to renounce on truth, but if they do... what do you think it'll happen?

He is pope, if the wicked relatio is passed and pope Francis approves it, then there is a NO doubt material heresy right there, then all the warnings given by all the true disciples of Christ and pope Benedict would be ignored, for the sake of the ANTIGOSPEL... a liberal gospel, a lie or lies proclaimed as truth... a "pastoral" poison.

Pope Benedict has drawn a line in the sand and it is a line made by his warning on the renunciation of truth and also the correction of his own words about divorce and re-married couples to get communion, this speaks LOUDLY, ask yourselves: How can there be a one true faith with priests rejecting the truth? If they give communion away, how can souls be saved with a lie? How can Benedict not do anything to save those souls? Exactly, the line has been drawn...

Think about it, how many would go to hell on that **lie**: communion to re-married couples, which is exactly "giving what is sacred to the dogs" (Mat 7:6). The Eucharist is going to be mocked with that lie, but what about the many priests going to hell by remaining silent and obeying iniquity by giving away the treasure of God, the Holy flesh of God.

Pope Benedict will obey God, Benedict will follow God, because he loves God and the Church and our Lord Jesus, our Blessed Mother will be watching and all the popes in heaven will be watching, martyrdom is coming and the other Joseph (Giuseppe), St Pious X prophecy[2] will be finalized, a prophecy in which he sees another pope with the same name as he running away from the Vatican (Joseph Ratzinger), will give his all for truth, and we only hope, that we could imitate his example.

God bless pope Benedict XVI, God bless the one true faith, praise be to God. Amen

Pennsylvania and Laudato Si.

The man seated in Peter's throne is visiting America in the wake of the presentation of His first Encyclica: "Laudato si"(1) which means "Praised be" in Latin.

Again in this work, this encyclica... has 37,784 words, that in the Literature sense... it's beautiful, tons of sugar pops and flowers all around.

The man seated in Peter's chair out of those 37,000 plus words mentions Abortion once... like in his strange teachings exhortation, Evangelii Gaudium. I don't know why so many people are raving about his "condemnation" to abortion, all faithful Catholics knows what abortion is, MURDER.

The Mothers who killed their child, the doctors, nuns, midwives, administrators of doom... are all assassins of the innocent, how many times have you heard him saying that? Never, and he has always established in few words that abortion is not progressive, "it is not progressive to eliminate a human life."(2) he has stated this many times, but one thing is what he says, how he says it and his deeds.

Bergoglio has said that in His autobiography "On Heaven and earth", also in Evangelii Gaudium and now in Laudato Si; but, he also has stated that we "talk too much about abortion, contraception and homosexuality" opening the door to murderers and giving them a second wind. 37,000 words of chocolate literature, but no proclamations of the reality, today Evil is good and what was once good now is evil... and today the world are calling what was evil a right.

"Woe to those who call evil good and good evil, who put darkness for light and light for darkness, who put bitter for sweet and sweet for bitter." (Isaiah 5:20)

Is there a better definition of liberalism in the bible than this one? Liberalism and Peter cannot co-exist, but anything nowadays is blurred and confusion is everywhere, tradition is shunned and worldliness is cheered; today tradition is called "going backwards" and priests are been persecuted for calling out the lies presented as truth by their own Bishops, and as it was mentioned before, St Francis of Assisi said this would happen:

"... Sanctity of life will be held in derision even by those who outwardly profess it..."[3]

The "Bishop of Rome" will walk to Pennsylvania, will preach his flowers and sugar pops as always, and will left out the evil of the world with pure omission, like he has done with Asia Bibi, when Ireland became Sodom, and about all those who are preaching to give the Eucharist to the unrepentant... Actually he has preach this, when he told that Argentine woman who is married to a divorced man, to get the Eucharist in a different Parrish and the Vatican has recognized that the call took place but its contents are not for the public... but we know, his bad fruits speak loud.

Nevertheless pray for his soul, NOT his intentions as our Lord wants us to pray for those who persecute us and even more... LOVE OUR ENEMIES (Mat 5:44), anything without love is a waste.

Antipope Francis. 10 reasons why pope Francis is an antipope, a false prophet (Mat 7:16)

First, Anti-pope according to the Baltimore Catechism #3 lesson12 Q 537, it means a pretended pope. The anti-popes were men who by the aid of faithless Christians and/or others, unlawfully seized and claimed the papal power while the lawful pope was in prison or in exile.

Pope Benedict is in exile... there is plenty of evidence that suggests he was pushed out the door, anyways, Benedict strongly believes that he still has a key from St. Peter, a spiritual key and he is praying for the Church in this dark times.

There is plenty of evidence which sustains that Francis papacy is not valid, beginning from heresies and even sacrilege while in Argentina (tango mass, let the 'curas villeros' give the Eucharist to irregular couples and the lobbying of his buddies for him to become pope and he even let the womb for hire of a transvestite and his male partner to be baptized with a big ceremony in a catholic temple) following with the invalidity of Benedict abdication, and ending with the continuous effort to put into oblivion sound doctrine and dogma. Let's begin...

10) History is not on Francis side.

There has been 37 antipopes in the History of the Church (1) and each time there's an antipope there's a true pope, there is a STRONG similarity with the history of popes Celestine V and pope Benedict XVI, they, were both push out the door by the cunning of evil men, as Benedetto Caettani convince pope Celestine V to abdicate, once Celestine abdicated then Benedetto (2) became the "pope" (how convenient, right?).

Pope Boniface VIII (Benedetto) persecuted Celestine in such a way that all his legacy was annulled by Benedetto, most of the things pope Benedict XVI did are being dismissed, ridiculed or rejected by Francis, and pope Celestine was imprisoned by Boniface, Benedict has said that he only comes out by invitation of Francis only... Boniface VIII and Celestine show us a precedent with remarkable similarities... today pope Celestine V is a saint and Boniface is not and his legacy ignored and forgotten.

9) Can the Holy Spirit preach what Francis has preached?

Can a priest be a homosexual and at the same time be a disciple of Jesus?

According to Francis yes... contradicting Benedict XVI, Holy Scripture and every council on this matter. On the question of a priest being gay, he said "who am I to judge" (3), but our forefathers have taught us, the pope is the supreme Judge and sodomy has been condemned throughout the history of the Church and Holy Scripture...

"The Congregation for Education issued a decision a few years ago to the effect that homosexual candidates cannot become priests because their sexual orientation estranges them from the proper sense of paternity, from the intrinsic nature of priestly being." (4)

How a homosexual priest can preach/teach the path of holiness when his own psych is problematic? Homosexuality is an abomination, a sin that cries for vengeance, a psychiatric illness (DSM II) and Francis has spoken like one of the world, not like he is a disciple of Christ, respect with no repentance is NOT in Holy Scripture, a true pope wouldn't dare to say that or even implied such a thing, but an antipope? yes...

"Do you not know that the unjust will not inherit the kingdom of God? Do not be deceived; neither fornicators nor idolaters nor adulterers nor boy prostitutes nor homosexuals nor thieves nor the greedy nor drunkards nor slanderers nor robbers will inherit the kingdom of God" 1 Cor 6:9-11

Love rejoices in truth (1 cor 13:6) how can you love someone by respecting them and not telling them the truth?, truth can set you free and point out your un-holy ways, without repentance and renunciation of sin Heaven cannot be achieved!!! Only people of the world has that with themselves, *"don't judge me"* BUT the spiritual man judges everything (1 Cor 2:15) and we HAVE to judge ACTS according to Holy Scripture to bring darkness to light:

"to open their eyes that they may turn from darkness to light and from the power of Satan to God, so that they may obtain forgiveness of sins and an inheritance among those who have been consecrated by faith in me." Acts 26:18

8) The hidden hand...

Pope Francis has demonstrated that he is the one pushing for total mockery of the Eucharist with his divorced and remarried pawn, Cardinal Walter Kasper, which, has been praised by Francis as a theologian doing "theology while kneeling" (5), then as he and others, back when pope John Paul II was alive, <u>he and others were defeated</u> on giving communion to the unrepentant.

"3. *Aware however that authentic understanding and genuine mercy are never separated from the truth, pastors have the duty to remind these faithful of the Church's doctrine concerning the celebration of the sacraments, in particular, the reception of the Holy Communion. In recent years, <u>in various regions, different pastoral solutions in this area have been suggested</u> according to which, to be sure, a general admission of divorced and remarried to Eucharistic communion <u>would not be possible</u>*.(6)

Henry the VIII wanted to divorce and remarried and many Saints suffered martyrdom because of this, a pope don't have the authority to change a revealed truth, in other words change the very words of Jesus Christ, in which He teaches about adultery.

"Everyone who divorces his wife and marries another commits adultery, and the one who marries a woman divorced from her husband commits adultery." Luke 16:18

"Therefore whoever eats the bread or drinks the cup of the Lord unworthily will have to answer for the body and blood of the Lord. A person should examine himself, and so eat the bread and drink the cup. For anyone who eats and drinks without discerning the body, eats and drinks judgment on himself." 1 Cor 11:27-29

Do you think Francis gets this? His fruits speaks for themselves, also, there is evidence that his beloved 'curas villeros' (7) gave the Eucharist to many, not stopping despite irregular marital situations and the infamous call to a woman married to a divorced man, telling her to get the Eucharist at a different Parrish, and there is no denial or acceptance of this sacrilege.

7) No conversion, no proselytism needed?

"Let your yes be yes and your no be no, <u>anything else</u> is from the devil." Mat 5:37

The ambiguity in all of his "teachings" are scary and Catholics who don't know their faith well are embracing it.

"Atheists who do good we'll meet there" is an unmistakable gigantic error and, he didn't want to correct his stance, on the contrary, you can find that he has been consistent throughout his life about contradicting the Lord's own words.

On Atheists: "I do not approach the relationship in order to 'proselytize', or convert the atheists; I respect him and I show myself as I am. Where there is knowledge, there begins to appear esteem, affection and friendship. I do not have any type of reluctance, nor would I say that his life is condemned..." (8)

"He said to them, "Go into the whole world and proclaim the gospel to every creature. Whoever believes and is baptized will be saved; whoever does not believe will be condemned." Mark 16:15-16

One thing Jesus commanded His first priests, first Apostles, firsts Bishops and first pope... go to the nations and proselytize...

Francis makes a distinction about proselytism as 'the PR of Catholicism' on that atheists quote in his book: on heaven and earth... he doesn't understand or cares, that same PR 'proselytism' was the reason many saints died in martyrdom...

"Atheists do good" bomb, is a slap in the face to every catholic that has persevere with sacrifices, sufferings and fear for the Lord. Atheists do good is just the tip of the iceberg... contradicting the Lord has been the theme for every antipope there is, but no antipope has ever spoke like him, so unopposed, never.

6) Disgust about tradition.

Catholic traditionalism is the performance of tradition by the faithful, it is viewed popularly as a person who practices the tradition of old, also called as orthodoxy.

"Therefore, brothers, stand firm and hold fast to the traditions that you were taught, either by an oral statement or by a letter of ours." 2 Thes 2:15

It is no surprise that an antipope rejects the teachings of our forefathers, but constantly mocking traditions that have created all the saints of our Church is shocking.

"I share with you two concerns. One is the <u>Pelagian</u> current that there is in the Church at this moment. There are some <u>restorationist</u> groups. I know some, it fell upon me to receive them in Buenos Aires. And one feels as if one goes back 60 years! Before the Council... One feels in 1940... An anecdote, just to illustrate this, it is not to laugh at it, I took it with respect, but it concerns me; when I was elected, I received a letter from one of these groups, and they said: "Your Holiness, we offer you this spiritual

treasure: 3,525 rosaries." Why don't they say, 'we pray for you, we ask...', but this thing of counting... And these groups return to <u>practices and to disciplines</u> that I lived through - not you, because you are not old - to disciplines, to things that in that moment took place, but not now, they do not exist today..." (9)

Practices and disciplines that every Saint went through and loved throughout 2000 years of tradition, without change. Despite the windows of the Church being opened in Vatican II, there hasn't been another Saint born into the world after 1965 like St Padre Pio or St Francis of Assisi, that right there says a lot... but tradition is the one too old and too rigid for a world demanding more and more freedom, worldly freedom that is, today truth is seen according to the context of the era we are living, when tradition doesn't yield to era, tradition is practiced how our forefathers and the bible told us so.

"Jesus Christ is the same yesterday, today, and forever." Heb 13:8

"...The other is the self-absorbed promethean neopelagianism of those who ultimately trust only in their own powers and feel superior to others because they observe certain rules or remain intransigently faithful to a particular Catholic style from the past..." (10)

Why block traditionalism when nobody is blocking the Charismatic movement? Traditional views are pelagian and self-absorbed, counting rosaries a sin, sad but true, Hypocrisy is the new pastoral arm of the top, but this man has been honest about tradition believers and their mindset: "Small-mindedness" (10)

5) Destruction of the papacy.

"I decided first thing to appoint a group of eight cardinals which will constitute my council. No courtiers but wise people and encouraged by my own feelings. This is the beginning of the Church with a non-vertical but horizontal organization." (11)

I can debate with any evangelical "when their church was founded and I can tell them when mine was founded" of course it was founded by Jesus Christ himself with Peter (Mark 16:18), but it is not about winning debates, because apostle Paul wants us to remain humble about us having and embracing the truth. Two thousand years ago Jesus receive the mandate from the Father and Jesus obeyed and did the same with Peter and the disciples, when Jesus was gone that same verticality that He received from the Father He taught Peter.

Two thousand years of verticality and this is the first pope to reject it and proclaim to the world a new way of running things, like a democracy is ran in any country, rejecting the red shoes of the fisherman, rejecting to wear the ring at times, rejecting the papal apartment to live in a hotel those are small potatoes compared to that admission, most Bishops, would love that because the more power most of them could crave... but...

"The floor of hell is paved with the skulls of bishops." St. Athanasius, Council of Nicaea, AD 325.

Dismissing the very way the Church has been ran since day one, says all about Francis...

4) Prophecy is against him.

"Rome will lose the Faith and becomes the seat of the Antichrist" Our Blessed Mother Mary said in La Salette, France September 19th 1846.

<u>In order for the Holy Temple to become corrupt it needs help from within</u>, someone will help the enemy for those purposes, so the elect could fall and the antichrist could be receive like a hero inside the Holy Temple.

"Let no one deceive you in any way. For unless the apostasy comes first and the lawless one is revealed, the one doomed to perdition..." 2 Thes 2:3

Someone will corrupt the Holy Temple and he'll have the appearance of a sheep while being a wolf.

St Francis prophecy is the most famous prophecy about this destroyer of the faith...

Pedro Regis from Brazil which his Bishop has declared those apparitions authentic, Conchita Gonzalez from Garabandal which saint Padre Pio said the apparitions were authentic, St Brigit of Sweden...etc.

3) Strange teachings.

"Do everything without grumbling or questioning..." Phil 2:14

Francis telling Catholics is alright to pray questioning God and asking why in the wake of the Philippines Typhoon. (15)

"Christians with the bible, Muslims with the Koran, with the faith of your fathers that it'll take you far." (16)

Those poor souls must have felt good

that someone that important is telling them that is alright to follow their false religion.

"There were also false prophets among the people, just as there will be false teachers among you, who will introduce destructive heresies and even deny the Master who ransomed them, bringing swift destruction on themselves." 2 Peter 2:1

Francis: "I am respectful of all new spiritual proposals, but they must be authentic and submit themselves to the passage of time, which will reveal if their message is temporary or will live on through the generations. Surviving the passage of time is the major gift of spiritual purity." (17)

Purity? And this man was selected pope with such a heresy written right there in his book on heaven and earth while he was bishop of Argentina? Well I guess it is nothing for Francis calling "pure" something that has passed the test of time forcing their believes with a sword and straight lies from Hell.

He has been "walking" with Jews, Muslims, Atheists, and all strange types of religions in Argentina and there is not one testimony of conversion from those false religions, not one.

He even called the old covenant of the Jews as <u>still valid</u>, when catholic councils, saints, prophets, apostles and even God Himself have said the old covenant was <u>broken</u>, if it is valid then they don't need Jesus, the New Covenant of Almighty Father.

'See, days are coming when I will make a new covenant with the house of Israel and the house of Judah, It will not be like the covenant I made with their ancestors the day I took them by the hand to lead them out of the land of

Egypt. <u>They broke my covenant</u>, though I was their master. But this is the covenant I will make with the house of Israel after those days. I will place my law within them, and write it upon their hearts; I will be their God, and they shall be my people. They will no longer teach their friends and relatives, "Know the Lord!" Everyone, from least to greatest, shall know me for I will forgive their iniquity and no longer remember their sin.' Jer 31:31-34

Francis told evangelical Tony Palmer <u>not</u> to convert to Catholicism (18) for the sake of an 'unity' agenda, it seems that Bishop Bergoglio doesn't mind the soul of his friend which would've had a more spiritual gain with the sacraments. But Francis said it:

"Proselytism is a solemn nonsense" (19) and Francis confirm that lie from hell again, with the 10 secrets to be happy he gave to Viva magazine "Don't do religious proselytism" [20]

2) Protestant theology.

"It is beautiful to think of this, to think of Heaven. All of us will be up there together, all of us! " [21]

Universalism, a protestant idea in which all of us are saved...

"How narrow the gate and constricted the road that leads to life. And those who find it are few." Mat 7:14

"So then, my beloved, obedient as you have always been, not only when I am present but all the more now when I am absent, work out your salvation with fear and trembling." Phil 2:15

If we all are going to heaven, then... why Catholicism?, why working so hard to stay true?, why the sacrifices? According to Francis we are going to heaven, like the erroneous protestant theology, "Once saved always saved."

"Of what things can a Christian boast? Two things: his sins and Christ crucified".(22)

Francis in his September of 2014 Santa Marta homily came up with this slap in the face to our Lord, the boasting of sins, like Martin Luther's dangerous theology "Be a sinner, and let your sins be strong, but let your trust in Christ be stronger" (23)

False prophet Martin Luther said one time, the Catholic mass (Tridentine mass) needs to be destroyed:

"Take away the Mass, destroy the Church." (24)

It feels since the persecution has increased to the Latin mass, that Francis goes by this false theology that the old mass needs to go. Sad...

1) Denial of Jesus.

"I believe in God, not in a Catholic God, there is no Catholic God, there is God and I believe in Jesus Christ, his incarnation. Jesus is my teacher and my pastor, but God, the Father, Abba, is the light and the Creator. This is my Being." (25)

Who is this Catholic God? All other religions believe in God but have no savior!!! Bergoglio is saying this himself and he believes in Jesus incarnation, that He is his pastor and teacher... but God is like another thing apart from Jesus... so again: Who is this Catholic God?

"No one goes to the Father except through Me" John 14:6

Jews believe in God, Jehovah witness believe in God, Buddhists believe in God, Muslims believe in God… but they have NO savior.

Ask yourself, Who is this Catholic God? The answer is: JESUS.

10 Secrets to be happy, no mention of Jesus anywhere in those secrets… When Francis said "Jesus pretended" it was another slap in the face of our Lord, not even joking and even less a pope, if he pretended to be angry at the apostles, he could've pretend, in other words: lie, at any time, denying such statement the Divinity of our Lord.

Not all is bad news

Not all is bad news for the "Bishop of Rome" and any of us hardheaded sinners, the Mercy of God is been poured in the world through the painful wounds of our Lord Jesus, this Mercy has no end, but it is for those who repent with contrite hearts and for us, to receive such a gift, we must embrace repentance in its fullness; now the "Bishop of Rome" needs to recognize before the Church his omissions and his intentions.

How many people have been misled with his omissions and false teachings? The whole world has been misled, he had the chance to proclaim the truth about Jesus in every opportunity and instead he proclaimed: "Don't do religious proselytism" going against the Holy word of Jesus when He told His Disciples...

"...Go and make disciples of all nations..." (Mat 28:19)

Anyways, the sole Judge of us all is our Lord and He doesn't deny Mercy for all who have true repentance and contrite hearts (Psalm 51:17), the first false pope or antipope was a man named Hippolytus, this man became a Saint[1].

Hippolytus (170 ad – 236 ad), became a false pope by declaring to be pope, when the true pope was Pontian, both Hippolytus and Pontian were exiled to the Sardinian mines, in the pre-Constantine era, Hippolytus saw how a Saint behaves, Pontian took all the suffering with love for God, Hippolytus repented and later was martyred by been dismembered by horses.

Hippolytus the antipope who became a saint, all because he recognized in time his error...

We all make mistakes, we all sin... but when people are deliberately trying to sell the Gospel for 30 coins, trying to give the pearl to the dogs (Mat 7:6), says it all about wolves in sheep clothing, the problem is that most Catholics don't know their faith well and embrace whatever is given to them, mostly because it seems logical or beautiful and everything he does and says sounds like flowers and sugar pops.

This man is loved and embraced by the world when every pope from the start of the Church has been hated by the world, so be careful and remain faithful to the one true bride of Christ, the Catholic Church.

> *"You adulterous people, don't you know that friendship with the world means enmity against God? Therefore, anyone who chooses to be a friend of the world*

becomes an enemy of God." (James 4:4)

Soon the man seated in Peter's throne will visit the United States and if repentance hasn't been found by him, he will continue to preach humanism, so open your eyes.

Still, it is our hope that through prayer and sacrifice, the same approach by Hippolytus is embraced by this false prophet, SO... let's pray for this man's soul to convert, NOT for his intentions.

"... Though your sins are like scarlet, they shall be as white as snow; though they are red as crimson, they shall be like wool. If you are willing and obedient, you will eat the good things of the land..." (Isaiah 1:18)

The way to the Golgotha

Many people right now all over the world is being persecuted, some are the victims that heaven needs to bring to righteousness the sinners, some others are martyrs whose blood is spilled to cleanse the church... many are killed in unspeakable ways, others raped, others slaved, others chopped like for the fun of an audience; tears and blood meet.

Jesus, is taking part in this new beating, this horrors are His, because He is the Master and Teacher, no one has suffered like He did, so... He must teach you to carry your cross to the Golgotha, but He never leaves you alone in this path, He... after a while, you will see Him carrying the cross with you and sharing your pain, which doesn't hurt like before, now watching the Master is worthwhile, His smile puts you almost in heaven, and when the time comes, you'll reach the top of the Hill with Him...

There, He will give you another miracle, as John listened the sweet sound of His Merciful Heart, you will too hear the Melodious sound of the waves of Mercy for you and the world, He will put you down to sleep like a Father does to His precious princess, put you in bed, which is the cross to sleep for a little while... Then you'll say:

"I wasn't worthy but you taught me to be yours, so please remember me when you come in to your Kingdom", and the lasts words you'll hear *"Amen I say to you, today you will be with me in paradise."*

The good pain of Christ, those by His friends who please Him in all His commands, those pains are His, because He never leaves you alone in this path of righteousness, which hurts so much...

His tears will encounter yours; since His death and resurrection all the pain of the ones that are His flock, that pain is His, you are not alone walking to the Golgotha.

His friends have walked with Him and suffered with Him, giving the Gospel by example and voice, many have believe because of those going to the Golgotha to share the good pains that only gives you glory in Him.

The most horrendous pain is the one that he shares with "no one", the pain that is inflicted upon Him by the people that are supposed to know Him, treason makes His sweat fall like blood on the ground.

Judas walked the earth with Him, saw Lazarus come out of the grave, saw lepers cleanse out of their miseries, he saw when Jesus walked upon the waters, Judas saw many evil spirits go out screaming from men, he went out with the 72 and proselytized, but instead took the 30 silver coins.

Many have seen small miracles and big ones as well, but they rather sell the Gospel, they have studied the lives of the saints and the teachings of our forefathers, but instead prefer some other strange teachings...

Thomas More died because Henry the VIII wanted to divorce his legitimate wife and re-marry, so because of this king, a traitor, Saint Thomas More was decapitated and his pains were with Jesus, the majority of the Bishops nailing Jesus to the cross again like Pharisees happened, and the procession to the Golgotha went with pure hatred for the sacred, instead the gain of power was placed, their own 30 silver coins.

The bad pains, the ones that makes Jesus suffered the stripes of open flesh, the thorns to the skull and one to His sweet eye... the big cross with all the spitballs and mockery, until the nails go in once again.

Proselytism brought us Saint Thomas More and many martyrs, St John the Baptist is weeping as many in silence are behaving like Herod, proselytism have brought the many who have shared the good pains with our Lord...

Today we need to make a decision, are we going to let the Lord taught us the way to the Golgotha and be a good disciple, or are we going to get our 30 silver coins...

Catholics were born for greatness, said pope Benedict XVI and this greatness lies in the cross which is hold by the nails impale to our flesh, proselytism is a good thing, Catholicism is a beautiful thing, when we give ourselves to Jesus the Master and Teacher... Don't let anybody deceive you, Jesus is that Catholic God and I believe in a Catholic God, and I hope you do too.

Blessings in our Lord Jesus Amen.

Last words...

In an interview with the Argentine daily newspaper, La Nación, he said among many things the following: 'Look, I wrote an encyclical, true enough, it was a big job, and an Apostolic Exhortation, I'm permanently making statements, giving homilies; that's TEACHING. That's what I think, not what the media say that I think. Check it out, it's very clear. Evangelii Gaudium is very clear'"[1]

For those who call his errors as his personal opinions, there... encyclical, exhortation and homilies... he is calling it "teachings", there's no way to escape the reality, we have been shown the door of hell: confusion, as the most beautiful thing, heresy and Peter cannot be.

At the beginning of this book we read the words of our Mother giving prophecy at La Salette on how the apostasy will cause the antichrist to seat inside the Holy Temple, some needs to corrupt the temple in order for the ruler of the world and the antichurch, to be seated in Peter's throne and declare himself as Jesus.

There are many prophecies approved by the Catholic Church today that Bergoglio is fulfilling, tons of contradictions of his "teachings" with the Holy word of God, this book could have tons of volumes and pages reflecting and showing each one of them.

The problem basically is how people embrace error so easily, how they don't question shaded teachings, we must Judge acts and all teachings given to us always... we don't know if the deceiver is in them. A lie with a truth is a lie altogether, this is why Catholics fail so much in our faith, because we don't read the bible as often as Christians do and even reading the catechism, despite us having the truth and beauty of the Church founded by Christ Himself.

It is also true that the consecrated who have to save souls, for fear of persecution stay silent...

We must never stay silent, those who are silent can miss martyrdom (the majority of the time) and martyrdom is heaven in a silver platter, those who are spiritual... understand this words, look at the true pope, Benedict XVI how much he is suffering in dry martyrdom.

Evangelii Gaudium is very clear Francis says, nope... it is confusing for those who are faithful and knows their faith, it opens the door for abortion, it proclaims a heresy when it says: "the old pact of the Jews is not broken" as many popes of the past, councils, saints and doctors of the faith according to Bergoglio are wrong, but IF the old pact isn't broken according to Francis, then Almighty Father is mistaken too as God in the book of Jeremiah 31:31-34 says it is broken, if the old pact isn't broken, then the Jews don't need Jesus as Savior, so yes Francis is wrong and with that and so many other things, the Francis effect have opened the door, bit by bit for Apostasy to happen.

LET US REMAIN FAITHFUL...

Remain faithful my brethren, St Athanasius was excommunicated and today he is a saint, because he, like how St Francis of Assisi said in his prophecy, remember? When he talked about those who accept error? St Athanasius didn't accept error, he proclaimed the truth of the Gospel by word, deed and he did it with love… there are many out there proclaiming the "truth" with a spice of hatred in it and it is so easy to hate… hate is from the devil and Love is from God, PLEASE… speak and live the truth of His Holy Word with love for those who are destroying you and all of us, it is too easy to flash the righteous anger card, but that is for God and those consecrated to Him: His servants, we the laity, are not worthy of barking out, we need to proclaim truth with love and RESIST with love… remain faithful with love and hope for martyrdom, dry or in death.

It is love that will save humanity and that Love is hanging from the cross.

May you stay faithful, may you resist the storm, may you proclaim the truth with Love and become a beacon for those in darkness... a big hug in Jesus Christ. Amen

Biography

First my testimony: Before my graduation occurred I was practicing pediatrics in the University's Hospital, I developed a severe bilateral pneumonia (breathing only through breathing devices), then a septicemia, my immunologic defenses weren't working because of a bone marrow aplasia caused by medications to reduce fever (the medication is called neomelubrina), under these conditions the doctors said that it would take a miracle to save me; many people prayed in many places in the world, **two different people saw Jesus watching me in my bed while in a coma** (7 days in coma)... after Jesus saved me from certain death, I had to go to New York to repair my trachea through surgery (over 15 surgeries), at the time I had a trachea stenosis caused by the artificial ventilator (breathing machine) I had while in coma.

After 3 years battling I finally recovered, but a permanent stoma was all that was left from all those surgeries making it difficult for me to go back to medicine again (the stoma was an open window for infections).

Jesus appeared to me in a dream and told me that He needed me to speak to the whole world about His Mercy and as proof of that, "NO light was going to be the next day", the next day there was no light!! The sky was dark all the gray thick clouds covered up above, the whole day was dark (I was in New York at the time), my father who was in Boston called me and I asked him about the conditions of the sky there, not knowing what was going on, he replied "it is all dark", then my wife called from Santo Domingo (Dominican Republic), and the same question was asked, she said "the sky is black and with much lightning", after that... I knew what I needed to do, I needed to tell everybody about Jesus Mercy...

I was born in New York the 21st of November 1972, son of Dr. Rafael Gonzalez and Amaury Frias. After my parents got divorced my mother took us to Dominican Republic, so I was raised in Santo Domingo, Dominican Republic; I found Jesus Christ in September 18, 1992 "All of my life never knew that Jesus was alive and I found Him in the Catholic Church." Started a family with Maria Tejada in 1997 my lovely wife, that same year I took medicine as a career at the Universidad Central del Este (UCE) in San Pedro de Macoris and graduating in 2005, right before graduation I got sick, due to the severity of my illnesses I couldn't practice as a doctor anymore due to the imminent danger of infections through my stoma, today I'm practicing my faith... advocating Jesus Mercy through the sweetness of receiving the Eucharist in the tongue instead of the hand in Saint Petersburg, Florida and hopefully soon I'll enter the Diaconate life with Jesus taking me there by His hand please pray for me my brothers and sisters for this to happen. Amen.

Bibliography

La Salette: http://www.thepopeinred.com/secret.htm

Introduction:
(1)http://www.usatoday.com/story/weather/2013/02/12/lightning-bolt-strikes-vatican-pope-benedict-resignation/1913095/

The prophecy of Saint Francis:

(1)http://www.novusordowatch.org/francis.htm

(*Works of the Seraphic Father St. Francis Of Assisi*, [London: R. Washbourne, 1882], pp. 248-250; underlining and paragraph breaks added.)

(*)http://www.periodistadigital.com/religion/vaticano/2014/10/02/non-e-francesco-un-libro-cuestiona-la-legitimidad-de-bergoglio-religion-iglesia-antonio-socci-papa-francisco.shtml

(**)http://chiesa.espresso.repubblica.it/articolo/1350910?eng=y

(***)https://fromrome.wordpress.com/2014/12/09/the-great-reformer-francis-and-the-making-of-a-radical-pope/

(2)https://www.catholicculture.org/news/headlines/index.cfm?storyid=10555

(3)http://www.catholicworldreport.com/Blog/2469/the_vatican_and_the_franciscan_friars_of_the_immaculate.aspx

(4) https://www.youtube.com/watch?v=GCchbeZT1lc

(4)http://chiesa.espresso.repubblica.it/articolo/1350910?eng=y

(5)http://www.traditioninaction.org/RevolutionPhotos/A487-BsAs-Homo.htm

(6)http://www.nytimes.com/2013/03/20/world/americas/pope-francis-old-colleagues-recall-pragmatic-streak.html?_r=0

(7)http://www.huffingtonpost.com/2013/05/22/pope-francis-good-atheists_n_3320757.html

(8)http://www.npr.org/sections/thetwo-way/2013/07/29/206622682/pope-francis-discusses-gay-catholics-who-am-i-to-judge

(9)https://www.lifesitenews.com/news/pope-kisses-the-hand-of-gay-activist-priest-allowed-to-concelebrate-mass

(10)http://www.theguardian.com/global/live/2015/may/23/counting-underway-for-irelands-referendum-on-marriage-equality

(11) http://www.massresistance.org/docs/gen2/14b/pride-week/about-pride-week/

(12)https://newwaysministryblog.wordpress.com/2015/05/14/nun-and-priest-join-with-other-irish-catholics-set-to-vote-yes-for-marriage-equality/

(13)http://www.ncregister.com/blog/tim-drake/the-myth-and-the-reality-of-ill-die-in-my-bed

(14) https://www.lifesitenews.com/news/chicagos-archbishop-cupich-communion-for-pro-abortion-politicians-is-a-good

(15) Evangelii Gaudium #47

(16) http://www.huffingtonpost.com/2013/09/19/pope-francis-gay_n_3954776.html

(17) http://www.usatoday.com/story/news/2015/01/19/pope-birth-control-comments/22017365/

(18) http://www.catholicherald.co.uk/news/2014/12/08/communion-not-the-solution-for-divorced-and-re-married-catholics-says-pope/

http://www.catholicherald.co.uk/news/2015/03/24/nearly-500-priests-in-england-and-wales-urge-synod-to-stand-firm-on-communion-for-the-remarried/

For those Catholics who should know more about their faith...

(1) http://romancatholicism.org/duty-resist.html

Blessed Catherine Emmerich

(1) Blessed Catherine Emmerich, AA II. 488.

(2) http://www.catholicnews.com/data/stories/cns/1403144.htm

(3)http://rorate-caeli.blogspot.com/2014/10/de-mattei-on-synod-relatio-need-to.html

Contradictions:

(1)http://en.radiovaticana.va/storico/2013/05/22/pope_at_mass_culture_of_encounter_is_the_foundation_of_peace/en1-694445

(2)http://vaticaninsider.lastampa.it/en/news/detail/articolo/francesco-francisco-francis-31406/

(2)https://www.lifesitenews.com/opinion/the-so-called-francis-effect-is-silencing-catholic-bishops-priests-and-lait

(3)http://www.rappler.com/move-ph/issues/disasters/typhoon-yolanda/44305-pope-francis-haiyan-tagle-philippines

(4)http://ncronline.org/blogs/distinctly-catholic/pope-francis-latest-bombshell-interview

(5) http://www.catholicnewsagency.com/news/pope-francis-use-intelligence-to-understand-signs-of-the-times/

(6) http://americamagazine.org/pope-interview

(7)http://www.bbc.com/news/world-asia-30890989

(8)http://www.nytimes.com/2013/07/30/world/europe/pope-francis-gay-priests.html?_r=0

(9) Evangelii Gaudium #247

(10)http://www.breitbart.com/national-security/2014/11/26/we-will-all-meet-in-heaven-says-pope-francis/

(11) final judgment http://www.romereports.com/pg155059-pope-s-audience-don-t-fear-the-final-judgment-jesus-will-be-at-your-side-en

(12)http://www.catholicnews.com/data/stories/cns/1403144.htm

Evangelii Gaudium opens the door for abortion:

(1)http://www.americamagazine.org/pope-interview

(2)http://www.vatican.va/holy_father/francesco/apost_exhortations/documents/papa-francesco_esortazione-ap_20131124_evangelii-gaudium_en.html

(3)http://www.cruxnow.com/church/2014/11/08/pope-makes-it-official-burke-is-out-at-vaticans-supreme-court/

Francis at the EU parliament:
(1)https://w2.vatican.va/content/francesco/en/speeches/2014/november/documents/papa-francesco_20141125_strasburgo-parlamento-europeo.html

(2)http://w2.vatican.va/content/john-paul-ii/en/speeches/1988/november/documents/hf_jp-ii_spe_19881128_deputati-danesi.html

False Mercy:

(1) http://www.nytimes.com/2013/07/30/world/europe/pope-francis-gay-priests.html?pagewanted=all&_r=0 Pope Francis telling reporters "Who am I to judge" on a Gay priest.
(2) If a man lies with a male as with a woman, both of them shall be put to death for their abominable deed; they have forfeited their lives.
(3) http://sspx.org/en/news-events/news/bishop-fellay-church-situation-catastrophic-5393 Bishop Fellay remarks on the Synod celebrated on October 2014.
4) "and you will know the truth, and the truth will set you free."

Pope Benedict draws a line in the sand...

(1) http://www.cardinalnewmansociety.org/CatholicEducationDaily/DetailsPage/tabid/102/ArticleID/3638/Pope-Emeritus-Benedict-XVI-Renunciation-of-Truth-Is-Lethal-to-Faith.aspx

(2) http://www.remnantnewspaper.com/Archives/2013-0228-siscoe-bishop-dressed-in-white.htm

Pennsylvania and laudato si:

(1) http://w2.vatican.va/content/francesco/en/encyclicals/documents/papa-francesco_20150524_enciclica-laudato-si.html

(2) Evangelii Gaudium #47

(3) http://www.novusordowatch.org/francis.htm

(*Works of the Seraphic Father St. Francis Of Assisi*, [London: R. Washbourne, 1882], pp. 248-250; underlining and paragraph breaks added.)

Antipope Francis: 10 reasons why Francis is an antipope (the false prophet)

(1)   http://en.wikipedia.org/wiki/Antipope

(2)   http://en.wikipedia.org/wiki/Pope_Boniface_VIII
(3http://www.catholicnews.com/data/stories/cns/1303303.htm
(4)   Pope Benedict XVI, light of the world p.152.
(5)   http://www.news.va/en/news/pope-francis-at-morning-consistory-session
(6)http://www.catholicnewsagency.com/resources/sacraments/eucharist/reception-of-holy-communion-by-the-divorced-and-remarried-members-of-the-faithful/
(7)http://chiesa.espresso.repubblica.it/articolo/1350910?eng=y
(8)   On heaven and earth by Jorge Mario Bergoglio and Abraham Skorka p. 12
(9)   http://rorate-caeli.blogspot.com/2013/06/pope-to-latin-american-religious-full.html
(10) Evangelii Gaudiim #83
http://w2.vatican.va/content/francesco/en/apost_exhortations/documents/papa-francesco_esortazione-

ap_20131124_evangelii-gaudium.html
(11) josephmaryam.wordpress.com Translation from the blog: Lumen Mariae, see the translation from Spanish to English word by word at: yucanation.blogspot.com
(12) Works of the Seraphic Father St. Francis Of Assisi, [London: R. Washbourne, 1882], pp. 248-250
(13) Evangelii Gaudiim #214 http://w2.vatican.va/content/francesco/en/apost_exhortations/documents/papa-francesco_esortazione-ap_20131124_evangelii-gaudium.html
(14) http://ncronline.org/blogs/francis-chronicles/latest-interview-pope-francis-reveals-top-10-secrets-happiness
(15) http://www.rappler.com/move-ph/issues/disasters/typhoon-yolanda/44305-pope-francis-haiyan-tagle-philippines
(16) http://www.romereports.com/pg155489-francis-to-refugees-christian-or-muslim-the-faith-your-parents-instilled-in-you-will-help-you-move-o-en
(17) On heaven and earth by Jorge Mario Bergoglio and Abraham Skorka p. 236
(18) http://www.novusordowatch.org/wire/palmer-not-convert-buried.htm
(19) http://www.repubblica.it/cultura/2013/10/01/news/pope_s_conversation_with_scalfari_english-67643118/
(20) http://ncronline.org/blogs/francis-chronicles/latest-interview-pope-francis-reveals-top-10-secrets-happiness
(21) http://rorate-caeli.blogspot.com/2014/12/for-record-in-week-of-papal-firsts-all.html
(22) http://www.news.va/en/news/mass-at-santa-marta-

why-boast-about-sins
(23) http://www.jesus-is-savior.com/False%20Religions/Lutherans/truth_about_martin_luther.htm
(24) http://www.stjosephschurch.net/deadly.htm
(25) http://yucanation.blogspot.com/2014/06/bergoglio-denies-jesus.html
(26) http://www.vatican.va/archive/ENG0839/_INDEX.HTM
(27) On heaven and earth by Jorge Mario Bergoglio and Abraham Skorka p. 220-221

Not all is bad news:

(1)http://catholicexchange.com/the-anti-pope-who-became-saint

Last words:

(1)http://www.catholicherald.co.uk/news/2014/12/08/communion-not-the-solution-for-divorced-and-re-married-catholics-says-pope/

www.ingramcontent.com/pod-product-compliance
Lightning Source LLC
Chambersburg PA
CBHW071502040426
42444CB00008B/1461